THOMAS HÖPKER

THOMAS

HÖPKER

Bryn Campbell

with

Thomas Höpker

COLLINS

THOMAS HÖPKER

by Bryn Campbell

Thomas Höpker

In the early 1960s a new generation of conspicuously talented photojournalists began to establish itself throughout Europe. British photographers like Ian Berry, John Bulmer, Philip Jones Griffiths and Don McCullin spring immediately to mind. Among their contemporaries in Germany, one of the most respected was Thomas Höpker.

Höpker's interest in photography began in 1950 when he was only 14 years old. His grandfather gave him an old plate camera and Höpker remembers, 'I felt the magic of this thing. I had my own darkroom and I got involved with the whole mystery of photography. Later, I bought my first 35mm camera and although I went to university and studied art history and archaeology, I never gave up photography; it was just a passion.' He spent 3 years at university but left without finishing the course, turning instead to a photographic career. His father was, and is, a journalist and so he had connections with the press world. After an early job with the *Münchner Illustrierte,* he began to work for *Kristall,* a magazine then known for its well displayed picture stories but now, alas, defunct.

Some of his finest photographs date from this period when he travelled widely for *Kristall* in the Middle East, South America, Africa and the USA (pages 8, 18 and 21). A portfolio of his pictures was published in *The German Photographic Annual 1965* and the editors commented that he was '. . . among the youngest photographers of the post-war generation and at the same time one of those with a most clearly defined style of his own.' These early pictures, like the best of his black and white work in general, have a simple directness of approach and a graphic strength that springs from precise composition and a feeling for shape and tonal balance (page 27). The simplicity of these images is rooted in awareness and not in naïvety.

Kristall was one of the very few German general-interest magazines that regularly used editorial colour in the early '60s and so, at a time when most photo-journalists were still shooting black and white, Höpker quickly built up a reputation for his colour essays. This stood him in good stead as the worldwide market for colour photography suddenly boomed.

'I am very much a commercial photographer', he said recently, 'I go where the assignment is and for the last 15 or so years the assignments have been in colour. Looking back at these early photographs makes me a little nostalgic and I begin to think that I would like to go back to black and white and do something very personal one day, if I have some breathing space and if I can do what I want. But perhaps I am not so sure about that; I'm very happy with colour now. I've totally forgotten the difference really. It's so natural for me to load a Kodachrome film into my Nikon and shoot. Maybe I would be a lousy black and white photographer now. It is not how I see today.'

Höpker has rarely been involved with hard news coverage. He was never considered a tough photographer who would go out and get the striking image of newsy events. But when he had to do this, he enjoyed it. 'I felt it was a great training for whatever you do later. It teaches you to react quickly, to go to the right position very fast, to handle your cameras and lenses instinctively. It's a good exercise.'

'Deep down I know when I've got a good picture or when I've shot roll after roll without taking anything important. Sometimes I keep shooting mediocre pictures and I know it but can't stop. There is such a nervousness about taking pictures and the clicking of the camera is like a drug.'

'Once I always tried to boil things down to essentials but now I'm slowly going away from the stark, simple composition, the graphic effect, in search of something more adventurous, more layers of reality in one picture, different things happening in one frame. I used to want to produce pictures with an immediate and distinct impact (page 17). Now I want to produce images that require a second, third, or even a fourth look, and slowly they reveal another aspect.'

'People sometimes compliment me on my colour composition but it isn't calculated; it is a subconscious thing, something instinctive. I don't compose consciously so much any more. Sometimes I just shoot away, blocking out all thoughts.'

'I can't pinpoint any major influence on my work. It has taken in such a wide variety of styles and subject-matter. Perhaps this has been a disadvantage in some ways—always experimenting, never happy with what I do, going from one extreme to another both technically and in subject-matter. I've taken very pretty, very calm pictures and also some rather gruesome photographs. Sometimes my pictures are very composed, very simplistic and clear, then again I have some less composed but exciting photographs. Sometimes the subject is more important, sometimes the composition and the imagery is more important.'

'I advise young photographers to go to museums and look at great paintings because one stores these images at the back of one's mind and when you are out there on assignment, suddenly these scenes pop back into your thoughts and it helps you in seeing reality.'

'It is a question of what intrigues you when you walk the streets. There is a certain amount of visual possibilities that connect with your personality. So if you have three photographers walking down the same street at the same time, they will see three different worlds. You cannot photograph anything that is not within you. If you don't have it within you, you don't see it.'

Höpker has never stayed on the staff of any magazine for longer than three to four years. He has moved on, keeping ties perhaps, but not bound by them. For instance, he had about three periods as a staff photographer for *Kristall* and also for *Stern,* for which he has worked as a staffer or freelancer from the mid-60s until today. [He has travelled the world on assignment for *Stern* and spent long periods for the magazine as a resident photographer in East Germany and New York (pages 23 and 31).] 'Somehow I always felt that it wasn't healthy to be a staffer for too long. You become a domestic animal. The editors think you are part of the system and they tend to send you on the same kind of jobs all the time. Also you have so much security—guaranteed salary, pension plan and so on—and I thought it wasn't good to be so pampered for too long.'

He has also worked on occasion outside the magazine field, producing five film documentaries for German television, some on his own and some with a reporter. Two of the films were on the famine in Ethiopia during the early '70s. He tried to take 'still' photographs at the same time but it didn't really succeed. He realized that he had to concentrate on one or the other, they call for such different ways of thinking. This period lasted about two years and he very much enjoyed it, particularly the creative possibilities working in the two added dimensions of movement and sound. 'But one reason I gave it up was that one gets into quite another world: the people who buy your films, use your material. It takes a quite different approach to get acquainted with these people. It's a very difficult world to get into. Also I felt uncomfortable with the fleeting aspect of films. You see a documentary on TV for half-an-hour and that's it; you'll never see it again perhaps, unless you show it to your friends. A photograph is something you can hold in your hand—it's there, you can look twice and see its strengths and weaknesses.'

'You cannot photograph anything that is not within you. If you don't have it within you, you don't see it.'

Thomas Höpker learned the rudiments of photography with a 9 × 12cm plate camera given to him in his teens by his grandfather. He soon graduated to a 35mm camera and he has stayed with this format ever since. Most of his work has been done with either Leica rangefinder models or Nikon single-lens reflexes, on which he increasingly depends.

He tries to carry the minimum of equipment, which makes it easier, he says, for him to concentrate. Normally he works with three camera bodies and five or six lenses: the 20mm, 28mm, perhaps 35mm, 50mm, 85mm and 135mm. If he is driving around in a car, he will probably also take a long telephoto lens and a super wide-angle. He has a tele-converter lens but very rarely uses it. Otherwise he makes use of all the lenses as necessary and has no particular preferences.

He has never been tempted to move into feature films. His background and his interests are solidly journalistic; what he wants to do is to document reality.

Yet one of his most exciting photographic projects had more to do with imagination than with reality. In 1976 he collaborated with the German sculptor Heinz Mack in creating and photographing a series of artworks that they set up in the Great Erg region of the Sahara Desert in Algeria and in the frozen fjords of Greenland, spending three weeks in each place (pages 44, 46, 47 and 48). At first, Mack intended to design objects on the spot or to introduce ready-made works into the landscape. Then Höpker was delighted to find that the sculptor 'was discovering what photography is all about, that is, reacting to situations. Once I saw some formation in the sand and I called to one of our two assistants to bring this and that and to put it just there. It was in the spirit of Mack's work and he liked the results, but it was a picture I made when he wasn't even there.'

'What fascinated me was that whatever pieces of art there are, only exist in these photographs. Sometimes in reality they only existed for seconds before the wind and sand blew over them. It was using photography as an art vehicle. I found it all very demanding and satisfying.'

Their book *Sculpture Safaris* was published in 1978, the same year that Höpker was appointed executive editor of the American edition of *Geo,* a German magazine from the same stable as *Stern*. He had been a photographer for over 20 years and he had reached a point where it had started to become repetitive. He felt that the new job was a great challenge. 'I've always believed I should try something I cannot do. The moment I know I can do something, that I am comfortable in it, it bores me. I thought it would give me more scope, added responsibility and I liked the idea of working with other photographers on a publication so unlike any other.'

However, after an eventful three years, American *Geo* was sold to another publisher and Höpker decided to return to being a full-time photographer. He had a difficult transition period for about six months, reacquiring the instinctive skills of handling his equipment, but he was soon very busy (pages 38, 39 and 40). By 1983 he was involved in producing three books—one on the former German colonies in Africa, China, New Guinea and the South Pacific; another on New York City; and one smaller volume on the theatre life in New York.

At *Geo* he was constantly exposed to the work of other great photographers and he was directly concerned in making decisions about the selection and use of their pictures. He hopes that this experience has broadened his understanding of photography and brought a new sophistication to his approach. He says, modestly enough, 'Looking at my old pictures, I find them a little simplistic now. I hope I've made a little progress in my work.'

On Photography

by Thomas Höpker

To write about photography in a profound way would mean, for any photographer, to write profoundly about his own life. Profound writing by anybody about his own life should, however, be avoided at all cost, unless there are exceptionally compelling reasons like extremely old age, unmatched literary brilliance or glamorous celebrity. Since I do not qualify in any of these areas, a few, not so profound and scattered observations must suffice here.

It is very obvious to me that the personal history and the lifestyle of any photographer shape the pictures he takes. Frequently I see images by other photographers which I adore, asking myself why I could not have taken this picture. But then I realize that picture-taking is a result of the way we live, the people we deal with, of what we read, what we eat, how we dress and what our dreams are. In a way every photograph we take is a self portrait. I believe it is impossible to take a photograph unless you had this picture already stored inside yourself. You simply do not see certain picture possibilities to which another photographer would jump immediately. But then he may have blind spots where you in turn react quickly and see very clearly.

The result is that only very rarely does one make real visual discoveries, does one invent totally new images or does one push open a door to a new alley that may lead to a fresh view. Time and again it has happened to me that, after I had taken a picture which I really liked, I discovered with dismay, sometimes days later, that I had only copied myself, that I had in fact re-taken a photograph which I had already snapped years ago in some other part of the world. The longer I work in photography the more I become aware of how limited my visual vocabulary really is.

How often does one really succeed to take a great picture? Maybe once every year—if you are lucky. The rest is high level routine, is hundreds of thousands of exposed frames. What a terrible misproportion between those kilometres of exposed film and that very rare truly fine image!

Editing my own material increasingly becomes a painful experience. To admit that so many frames are not perfectly exposed, not totally sharp or (worse) rather bland pictures is not too pleasant a process. A hundred rolls from a long trip may finally be reduced to a hundred frames and then I feel the itch to boil down that number even further to just a handful of pictures. Having reached that stage it would come as a wonderful relief to reduce this number to zero and send an empty carousel tray off to the assigning editor along with a letter:

'Dear friend, I hope you are not too disappointed to receive the enclosed amount of zero colour transparencies which I brought back from my trip to Outer Mongolia. I am sure you will understand that this trip did not yield any important photographs and I know that you, more than anybody else, understand that there are too many photographs in our world anyway. So why add to that pile of superfluous images? I had some very pretty ideas for several magnificent pictures while I was travelling. I would have taken them if only a less than perfect reality had not been in my way. It might actually be nice to describe these untaken photographs to your readers but on the other hand I am sure that most readers will be so grateful to see some empty, white pages in your magazine. It will come as a relief to them after having seen all those mediocre photographs and all the excited clutter of texts and graphics on the preceding pages.'

'I am sure, your accounting department will understand that I had considerable

'How often does one really succeed to take a great picture? Maybe once every year . . . if you are lucky.'

continued on page 56

7

Nun and leper, Ethiopia, 1963

Dayak children, North Borneo, 1965

Famine in India, Bihar province, 1967

Starving man and sacred cow, Patna, India, 1967

Temple dedicated to rats, Deshnoke, India, 1967

Woman of the Konibo Indian tribe, Peru, 1962

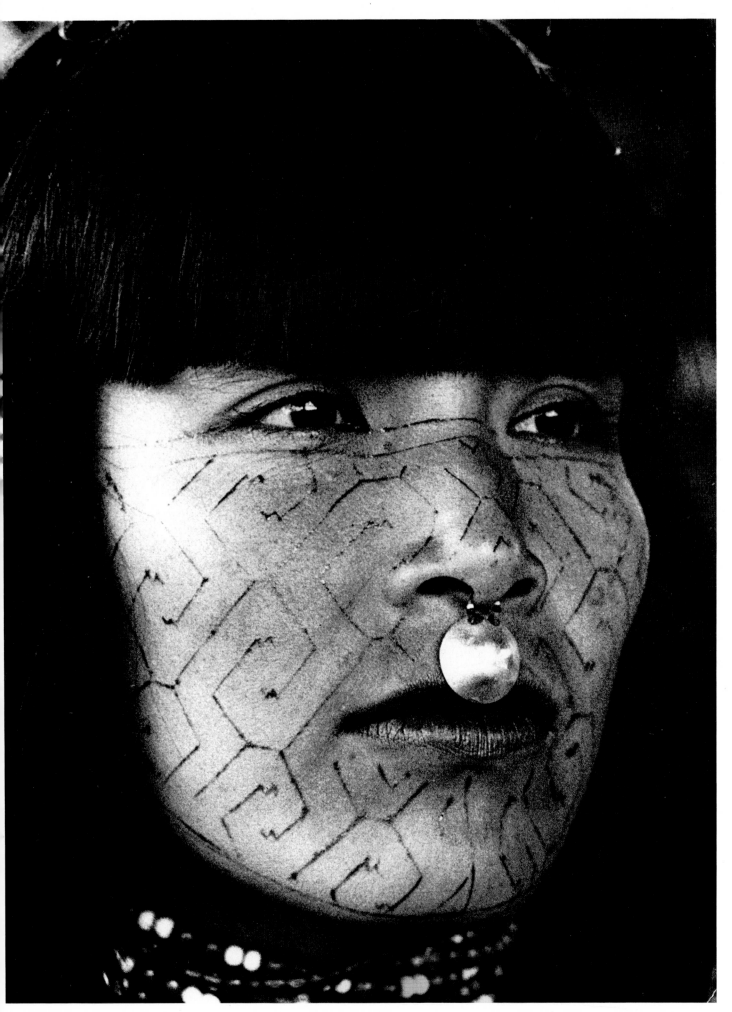

Konibo woman, Peru, 1962

Duchess at a reception, Jerez, Spain, 1966

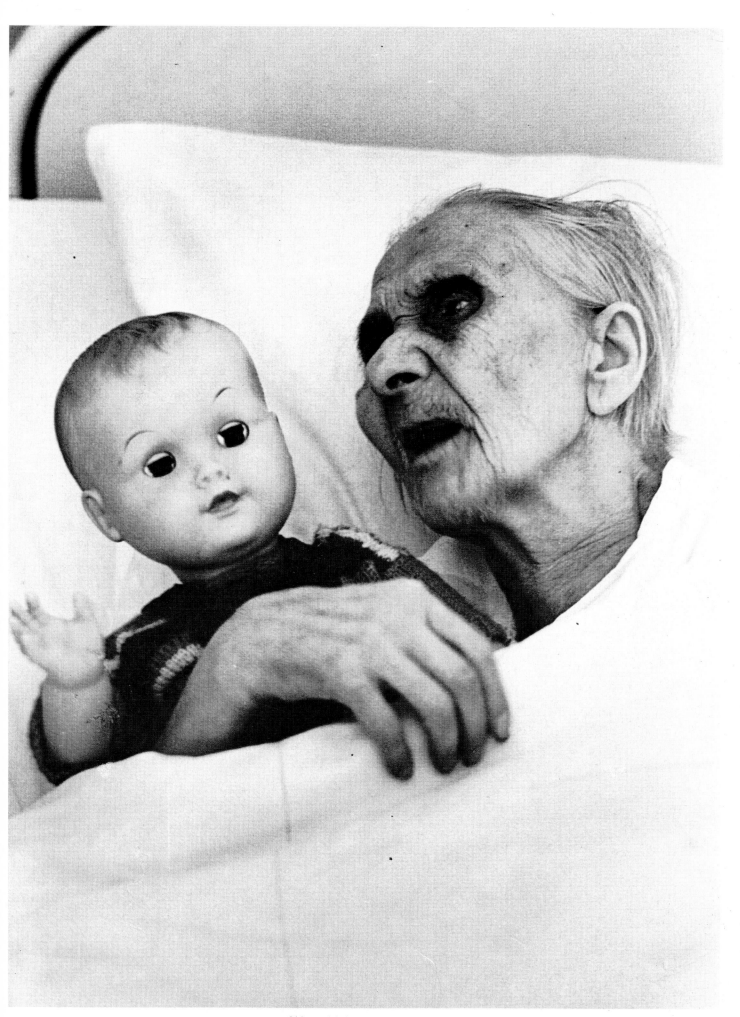

Old people's home, Hamburg, 1965

Tourists at the Pyramids, Egypt, 1963

People in Red Square, Moscow, 1965

Billboard, Alabama, 1964

Crippled beggar, Quincy, Illinois, 1964

U.S. war veterans, San Francisco, 1964

Parade in East Berlin, 1974

American football training, Butte, Montana, 1964

Muhammad Ali, Chicago, 1966

Military parade, Bonn, 1968

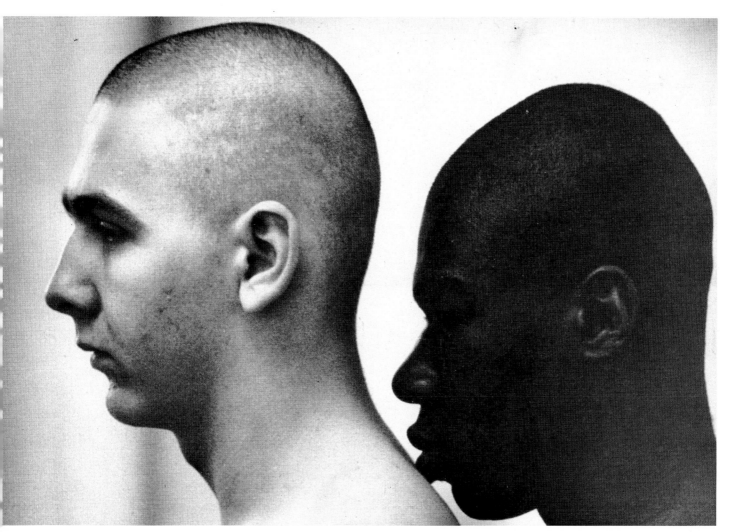

U.S. Marines in training, Parris Island, USA, 1970

Indian woman at the market, Mexico City, 1968

Peasants carrying wild flowers, San Cristobal, Mexico, 1968

Employment office, San Cristobal, 1968

Damaged house, Cottbus, East Germany, 1975

Strawberry growing, Galilee, Israel, 1973

Ricefield, Central Valley, California, 1982

Hotel room in Kyoto, Japan, 1977

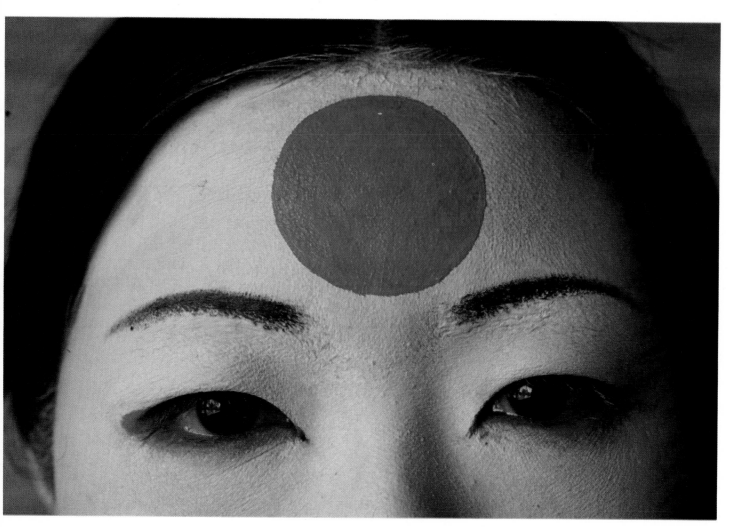

Japanese girl with traditional make-up, 1977

The garden of desires, Kyoto, 1977

Ceremonial umbrellas, Tokyo, 1977

Central Park, New York, 1981

Soho Street, New York, 1982

Peace gathering, San Francisco, 1982

Advertising, Los Angeles, 1978

Small girl at a Shinto procession, Tokyo, 1977

Mural, Los Angeles, 1978

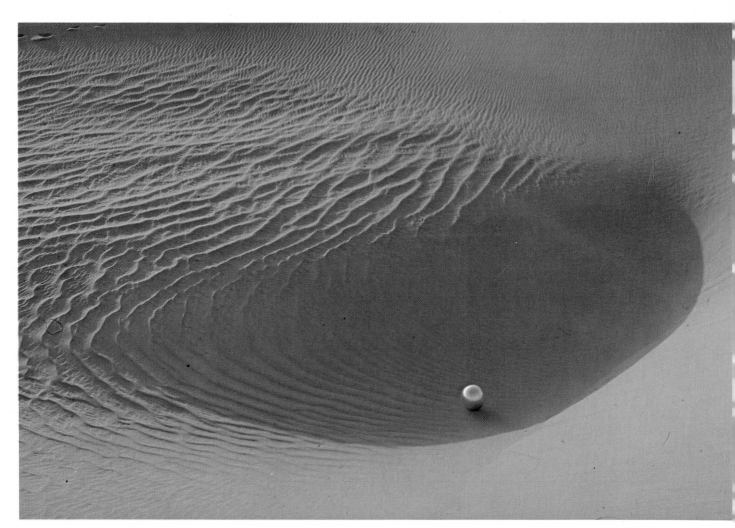

'Sculpture in the desert', Algeria, 1976

Horsemen in the desert, Algerian Sahara, 1976

'Sculpture in the desert', Algeria, 1976

'Sculpture in the desert', Algeria, 1976

'Sculpture on ice', Greenland, 1976

Midnight sun, Greenland, 1976

Ghost town, Bodie, California, 1977

Japanese roofs, Kyoto, 1977

Sydney Beach, Australia, 1971

Japanese umbrellas, Tokyo, 1977

Village on Achill Island, Ireland, 1972

Central Park in winter, New York, 1980

continued from page 6

expenses for flights, meals, hotel and film in Outer Mongolia. I hope you will assign me to go to some other exciting country soon, since I just love thinking about taking pictures for you! With best wishes, yours, T.H.'

Bad pictures can make me feel sick and the worst for me are those pretentious photographers who seem to postulate that only very bad pictures are great art and that's what important museums should hang on their walls. If I understand them right, some of these photo artists feel that an empty and bland society can only be portrayed in empty and boring images. But who is more boring here—the subject or the photographer?

I have always felt uncomfortable to see photographs hanging on gallery walls framed and spotlighted as a backdrop for a wine and cheese carrying crowd. I have always believed that photography is a means of communication, that is best displayed in a newspaper or a magazine to be discarded the next day. I have always been suspicious of photographs that seem to shout from a wall: 'Look at me, what a wonderful photograph I am!'

Yes—imperfection makes me sick, especially in my own photographs. But then —total perfection will eventually bore me to tears. Yes—I love a perfect and balanced composition. Form has always been very important to me. But more and more I find that form should not be overpowering. In many a photograph, form, composition and colour just camouflage the fact that the photographer had nothing much to say. Oh, what a fine picture! But who needs it? What does it communicate? George Simenon once said, 'When I write a novel, I write it all the way to the end as good as I can. And then I sit down and take out anything that resembles style.'

To tell a good story, to communicate an important thought, that's what photo-journalism is all about. And that should be done directly and simply. Not too much style, please!

'I have always felt uncomfortable to see photographs hanging on gallery walls . . . as a backdrop for a wine and cheese carrying crowd.'

A pleasant May sun warms Saint Peter's Square in Rome. In the background next to the colonnades, a small white figure becomes visible above the heads and outstretched hands of the crowd. Josef Hartmann, 60, a German railway employee from the small Frankonian town of Moemlingen, is well prepared for that moment. He has loaded his Agfa Silette camera with Agfa CT-18 slide film; exposure time, opening and distance are all set. As the Pope passes close by, Josef Hartmann and his wife Erna get lucky enough to touch the hand of the Holy Father, but in all his excitement Hartmann forgets to lift the camera. Only after the Pope-mobile has passed does he manage to take a picture, but he sees no more than the back of John Paul in his viewfinder. When Hartmann takes his camera down to check the exposure setting, he hears a few bangs; there is turmoil. Stuck as he is in the crowd, he tries to grasp what has happened, does not take any more pictures, is shocked as he finally understands—someone has shot the Pope.

The Hartmanns stay in Rome for three more days. Back at home, their vacation films are mailed to a lab. On Sunday, May 24, when their son Wolfgang comes to visit, eleven days have passed since the assassination attempt in Saint Peter's Square. After the family dinner, father Hartmann begins to project his vacation slides. There is Erna Hartmann on the Spanish Steps, photographs of Saint Peter's basilica, even the frame with the Pope in focus and correctly exposed. Suddenly Wolfgang Hartmann discovers what his father has not yet noticed: in the crowd, to the left of the white-clad figure, there is a man with a hand gun. The Hartmanns get really excited when they finally realize what the Agfa Silette has captured. This is the only photo which shows Mehmet Ali Agca, the Turk, in the very moment of the assassination attempt. His face is clearly visible.

What does a railway employee in Moemlingen do with a really sensational photograph? Nothing, if he can help it. Josef Hartmann is very much opposed when his son suggests selling the picture to the press. But Wolfgang stubbornly insists and finally tries his luck with *Stern, Quick* and *Bunte.*

None of the magazines seems very interested. The shooting of the Pope has faded like the snow of yester-year. All existing photos have already been printed. But then, three weeks later, *Quick* magazine agrees to run the picture. It is not before autumn that Hartmann gets his transparency back. He hands it over to DPA agency who starts to distribute the picture worldwide. *Time* magazine shows the photograph as a curiosity in its 1981 year-end issue. Altogether, Hartmann has made something over US$1,000. He is still surprised that people have made so much fuss about his chance hit.

Only six weeks prior to the shooting in Rome, a very similar story occurred in Washington, D.C. Sebatiao Salgado Jr, 33, a Brazilian photographer and member of the Magnum group, feels frustrated. For the last three days he has been trying to take pictures of President Reagan. But all his credentials, even his good connections through the *New York Times Magazine,* for which he is on assignment, do not get him past the security guards in the White House.

In the afternoon of March 30, Salgado sees Ronald Reagan for the first time. The President is speaking at the congress of the Construction Worker's Union at the Washington Hilton. It soon becomes all too clear to the photographer; this is a routine job and there is hardly a chance to grab a decent picture. But anyway— one never knows—he loads two fresh rolls of Kodachrome into his cameras while he waits outside next to the presidential limousine.

When Reagan finally emerges from the exit door, what happens next is every seasoned pro's subconscious dream and nightmare: shots ring out, people wrest-

The Glass-eyewitnesses

Photojournalists and their reality

by Thomas Höpker

. . . the only photo which shows Mehmet Ali Agca in the very moment of the assassination attempt.

57

ling, people wounded, ambulances, police. After a brief initial shock Salgado reacts instinctively. He shoots away with his three Nikons, closes in, becomes part of the scene. When everything is over he has exposed 3 Ektachrome and 2 Kodachrome films, 180 frames in all.

Ten minutes after John W. Hinckley has fired at Ronald Reagan, Salgado calls the Magnum office in New York, and triggers one of the fiercest bidding wars in the history of photography. No one has seen the pictures yet, but the Magnum offices in New York and Paris soon resemble a commodities exchange. The major magazines enter their bids. When at 8 p.m. his films are returned from the lab, Salgado knows he has reacted as a professional. Only his first four frames are blurred; all the rest is perfect.

The next morning Rosemary Wheeler, representative of Magnum in New York, learns that four European magazines have already put up a total of US$45,000. She calls James Kenney, picture editor of *Newsweek* and asks for $75,000 for the American exclusive rights for the Salgado take. *Newsweek* agrees—this is the highest fee ever paid by a magazine for one set of pictures. Just a little later *Time* magazine calls, and offers to pay as much as $100,000. But it's too late. The deal has been made. Salgado and Magnum may have totalled as much as $180,000 through worldwide sales.

Most of the time a reporter's luck is somebody else's misfortune. The Egyptian photographer Makram Gad El-Karim got 'lucky' because he stood at the right spot with the right lens and a still half-empty roll of film in his camera when President Sadat got killed in October 1981. The take sold for $50,000. Wedding photographer Hans E. Wendt was 'lucky' too—he had his camera with him on his way to church when a Boeing 727 collided with a small aircraft above San Diego in 1978. The assassinations of John F. and Robert Kennedy, the mass suicide in Jonestown, the burning monk in Saigon, the sinking of the Titanic, the Hindenburg exploding at Lakehurst: these mishaps, catastrophies and crimes are stored as vivid images in our brains.

Ever since the first newsphoto was made 140 years ago—a panoramic view of Hamburg after the big fire of 1842—photojournalism has excelled in depicting horrors. The pleasant, the ordinary rarely make the news.

Given the demand for sensational photographs, everyone regards press photographers as an overbearing lot, as mercenaries in the pay of public curiosity; ever in pursuit, flashgun at the ready, of the unsuspecting victim. Armed to the teeth with the tools of their trade, they elbow their way through the crowd, trampling on the gardens of the famous, jamming their feet into half-closed doors and lying in wait for the widow before the still-open grave. But are press photographers really only cold 'glass-eyewitnesses'? Certainly, in talking to top photographers, the dilemma of this profession comes out: how can artistic sensitivity be reconciled with the necessarily tough job of the reporter?

Philip Jones Griffiths, despite being President of the Magnum group and having produced the most terrifying book of photographs on Vietnam ever seen and despite having been a reporter for twenty years, still has difficulty in photographing people in the street: 'If you are sensitive enough to see unusual images, you are also sensitive and shy when you have to stick your lens into some stranger's face.' Griffiths now knows instinctively how far he can go on each occasion. He has learned to interpret the body language of the people around him and achieves what he wants by gentle persuasion. 'So far I have never been attacked. No one has ever thrown me out.'

'Are press photographers really only cold "glass-eyewitnesses"?'

Volker Hinz, on the staff of the magazine *Stern,* is regarded by his colleagues as a tough nut who never takes no for an answer. Yet he says of himself, 'Deep down, I'm a shy person. It costs me a great deal of psychological effort to have to elbow my way through a crowd of photographers to get to the front. But what can you do? I have to get the best picture at all costs.' Hinz also knows that cold routine can be dangerous. 'I have to work up enthusiasm for each new job. I have to become more open and sensitive. I have to be prepared for the unexpected.'

Leonard Freed has demonstrated exceptional courage in an impressive book on the New York police. Yet in spite of some twenty-seven years' experience, he still has scruples when he has to ring a doorbell or talk to a stranger on the phone. 'I remember a mine disaster in Belgium. I had to take pictures of a family in which the husband and two sons had just died. Where did I find the brutality to do something like that?', asked this respected Magnum photographer.

Sometimes even a hardened pro can't go all the way. Matthew Naythons, an American physician and photographer, hates to recall the visit of US 'First Lady' Rosalynn Carter to the refugee camps of Thailand in 1979. 'Some photographers were literally trampling dying babies to get better shots.' Appalled, he packed his cameras and returned home without pictures. Eugene Smith, the late grand master of concerned photography, had to face a different problem while he was working on his famous story on mercury poisoning in Minamata, Japan. Talking about how he took one of the most celebrated pictures—a mother bathing her crippled child—Smith said, 'I shot 5 to 6 frames. Then I had trouble focusing. My eyes had filled with tears.'

'Some photographers were literally trampling dying babies to get better shots.'

Smith suffered frequently for his photographic and humanistic beliefs. In Japan he was severely beaten by thugs hired by the chemical plant whose environmental negligence he had documented. As a war correspondent in the Pacific in 1945 he was severely wounded and needed 32 operations. 'More photographers than generals died in Vietnam,' says Magnum photographer Raymond Depardon. Some 30 cameramen perished in this most photographed of all wars. 'If your pictures are not good enough, you were not close enough,' said war photographer Robert Capa, who got killed when he stepped on a land mine in Indochina in 1954.

Being up close—that is the curse but also the strength of the photographic medium. A reporter can do his writing from a safe distance behind the lines, gather information second hand or even by sorting through files. A photographer has no choice; he cannot take photos from behind a desk, he has to be right where the action is. This requires a special temperament.

'Occasionally photographers are a little crazy, and almost always they are obsessed,' writes *Time* magazine in a story on photojournalism in January 1982. Good photographers seldom fit the corporate mould. They can be a nuisance; most are emotional. Many of them are politically motivated, have a soft spot for the downtrodden, are liberals, since every day they have to cross the line towards poverty, sickness, mischief or simply towards the everyday lives of the common mass. Photography is blue collar work, it means dragging heavy equipment around, rain or shine, in heat and cold; it means hanging out at street corners—certainly not a noble profession.

The closer a photographer has got to his subject, the more the viewer of the resulting picture will be convinced that he's actually looking at a slice of reality. Photography is considered proof that something has in fact happened. If a tree falls in the forest and no one is there to hear it—does the tree make a noise? This ancient conundrum could be re-worded today: Has an event really taken place, if no one was there to photograph it? The horrors of the Gulag archipelago have been masterfully described on thousands of printed pages. But still they remain somehow distant and bodyless—they were never photographed. The nightmares of Auschwitz or Dachau, on the other hand, seem shockingly real. Pictures of the indescribable, projected sharply into our memories, are painful proof of what happened there. The genocide in Indonesia, in which hundreds and thousands of Communists were killed after 1965, remains basically an historical footnote for us westerners, just as the misery of those persecuted in East Timor today. Nobody was there recording it in pictures. It is almost as if it never really happened.

So we are all convinced that photographs are evidence. But how often has this medium deceived us! The camera's black box still holds some of the old magic and carnival illusion. Truth? Reality? They are probably present in those spontaneous and artless pictures of the Pope and Reagan shootings. Here the event creates the image. In Saint Peter's Square, the picture drops into the Agfa Silette almost by itself, and even the pro in front of the Washington Hilton is just able to react breathlessly, does not find time to compose, that is, to manipulate.

These pictures are real documents. But how many photojournalists are lucky enough even once in their lifetimes to witness such an extreme event? We normal photographers have to cope with everyday life and a lot of dull routine. There is no other way—we have to improve on reality, to hype up the all-too-common until it becomes un-common and thereby interesting.

Just beautiful isn't enough—the image has to be breathtaking. Strange isn't enough—weird, bizarre, far out is what is needed. Otherwise, no one will notice the picture. So we are forced to improve situations by gentle direction. We use extreme lenses to distort, exaggerate, condense, isolate. We stalk the unusual lighting, the surprising moment.

Magazine readers are a hardened audience. They have already seen too many strong pictures; they are numb. 'In a sense, photojournalists today are competing against all the news pictures that have ever been taken,' writes *Time*.

'This job becomes more and more difficult the longer you stay with it,' complains Mary Ellen Mark, the eminent New York photographer who has found her strongest pictures in extreme human situations, in insane asylums, brothels, old age homes. 'I have to uncover the innermost secrets of people. I have to show extreme reality.' But does she actually extract reality, whenever she strips people down to their souls with the merciless sharpness of her lens? We'd better get used to it: very few photographs are reliable documents. The camera is about as objective as a typewriter or a painter's brush. The best photographs and picture stories are reality seen through a temperament, seen by photographers who are authors with their very own styles, personal preferences and animosities.

But photographers don't deliver a finished product anyway. Between the camera artist and his public stand the editors, and the art directors, the image maestros who orchestrate the fortissimos. Out of a thousand frames they filter the one dozen top images they deem worthy to print. Out of the second reality created by the photographer they form a third reality on the page. 'The camera cannot lie; but it can be an accessory to untruth,' writes Harold Evans, former editor of the London *Sunday Times*. 'Castro is, depending on the editor's whim, a scowling belligerent or the idol of his people.'

Fortunately it is considered more and more old-fashioned or even outright unethical to 'improve' photographs through retouching or photomontage. These manipulations are a relic from early days of photography, when painter-

'Photojournalists today are competing against all the news pictures that have ever been taken.'

photographers tried to beautify their not-so-perfect images. Legendary stories are told of the publisher of *Bunte Illustrierte* who is said to have called his retoucher when he saw a colour take on Austria in layout. 'I want that Danube to be blue,' he demanded. Even *Stern* magazine became exposed to professional ridicule recently. In an underwater picture story, a daring diver could be spotted amidst a large school of shark. Readers had reason not only to admire the man's audacity but also his unconventional technique of survival—the retouching artist had halfway successfully painted the diver into the picture but had forgotten to equip him with a diving tank!

Though pictures are less and less often doctored or falsified for added effect or even propaganda, one thing becomes clear: editing picture magazines is always a process of selection. Choosing from an abundance of photographs naturally reflects the personalities of photographer, editor, art director. It is a continuous search for the strongest effect. This is why the world looks so splendorous in our best magazines.

Many photos vacillate like soap bubble rainbows. They change their meaning depending on how they are played against other pictures or how they are captioned. In 1968, I photographed how a few courageous young men toppled the big Soviet star from a town hall in Czechoslovakia. Years later I found that same photo in the December issue of a Catholic paper with a caption reading: 'Everywhere Christian believers decorate public buildings with a Christmas star.' The meaning of the picture was reversed, but nobody noticed; the photograph didn't mind.

Manipulation of photographs and harassment of photographers are an established power ploy of totalitarian regimes. The Polish military government knew only too well what it did, when it kept journalists and photographers from working, beginning in December 1981. Reports on the Polish tragedy, documented only by clumsy amateur photographs, have never reached the intensity of picture stories about the uprising in Hungary or Czechoslovakia. But photography is also censored and suppressed every day in papers and magazines in our western democracies. Any picture that will not fit well into the policies of a publishing house are eliminated according to an uncodified but nevertheless extremely sensitive system of internal censorship. The picture editor of *Bild,* Germany's big conservative paper, would never consider a picture showing an obviously happy East German communist. Just as on the other side of the fence *Neues Deutschland* would certainly not show a smiling miner of the Ruhr. But even stronger and probably more effective than ideological censorship are the forces of the marketplace and its functionaries who finally decide what their readers will see and what they will not.

'That might, say the publishers, have a bad effect on the advertisers.'

As if they were under secret orders, American magazines of the eighties rarely publish pictures of poverty or racial tension. That might, say the publishers, have a bad effect on the advertisers. Cosmetic monotony is the result. And since official Washington tends to play down minority or social problems anyway, what is not being photographed just does not exist.

Too much pressure can turn photojournalism, the dreamjob, into a nightmare for some professionals. David Burnett, 35, one of the busiest, spent only 90 days at home in New York in 1982. He practically lived in hotels and on airplanes. 'The other day, the picture editor of *Time* called me,' he said. 'He had a dream assignment for me—two weeks in the Caribbean. I never had a more terrible job. Six islands in fifteen days. On day thirteen I finally sat down at a swimming pool with a tuna sandwich for two hours. Everything else was sheer murder.'

While looking at old photographs we sometimes become nostalgic. How much loving time did early photographers like Atget or Stieglitz spend setting up their tripods. With how much relaxed dignity have Kertész or Cartier-Bresson observed other people! Ernst Haas has watched his great colleague and friend Henri Cartier-Bresson at work. 'You don't have the feeling that here is somebody who is thinking in terms of pages and layouts. He just seems to melt into the situation he photographs. There he stands in what in ballet is called the "sixth position", observing and photographing—never bending over too deeply, never on top of a table or underneath; certainly never on his stomach. His view is that of a gentleman who would never take distorting poses while working in order to improve a photographic angle. The eyesight of a normal man standing and walking is enough.'

For us, who are always bending over backwards to effectively frame some super reality, this sounds like a tale from the good old days. But many of us suffer from the pressures of the medium and reach for other ways. Lord Snowdon admits, 'In the past I have taken terribly exaggerated pictures. Today I try to be more simple. I would not mind even to take a boring picture if it only holds the truth about a person.' Leonard Freed says, 'It's strange, you go out again and again. You still think, that great picture might just wait for you around the next corner. And when you really find it occasionally—those are the moments when you suddenly get high.'

How does one feel having run around the world with a camera for some forty years? Eberhard Seeliger and Hilmar Pabel, two veterans of German photography, agreed when they once met in the reporters' room at *Stern* magazine, 'You should live to be 300 to digest all you have experienced in this job.' And Volker Hinz, the young *Stern* photographer, sometimes feels like the old American Indian in the story who, for the first time in his life, is taken for a ride in an automobile. For three hours the car speeds along the highways. At his arrival the Indian insists on sitting down and resting for three hours. 'I have to wait,' he says, 'until my soul has caught up with me.'

Bibliography

Books

Yatun Papa (book about a German doctor who worked among the Indians), Kosmos, Stuttgart, 1964.
Horst Janssen (about a German artist), Hamburg, 1969.
Berliner Wände (on the ruined walls of East Berlin), Hanser, Munich, 1976.
Leben in der DDR (life in East Germany; text by Eva Windmöller), Stern Books, Hamburg, 1977.
Sculpture Safaris ('Expedition in künstliche Gärten'), Stern Books, 1978.
Vienna, Great Cities Series, Time-Life Books, Amsterdam, 1979.
The New York Story, Geo Books, Hamburg, 1983.

Exhibitions and awards

1954 and 1956 Photokina Prize, students' category.
1965 Exhibition at the Kunst and Gewerbe Museum in Hamburg, together with Stefan Moses, Max Scheler and Eberhard Seeliger.
1968 Cultural award of Deutsche Gesellschaft für Photographie.
1973 Group exhibition in London.
1976 Bundesverdienstkreuz (Distinguished Service Cross of the German Federal Republic).
1978–80 Exhibition of dye transfers of Heinz Mack and Höpker's expeditions, shown in Hamburg, Munich, Berlin, Vienna, Paris, New York, Washington and Tokyo.

Chronology

1936
Born in Munich on 10 June.

1950
First photographic experiments with an old 9 × 12cm plate camera and in the darkroom.

1956–59
Studied art history and archaeology in Munich.

1960
Joined the *Münchner Illustrierte* as a press photographer.

1962
Joined *Kristall* magazine in Hamburg.
Travelled to the Middle East, Brazil, Peru, Egypt, Ethiopia, New York and Iran.

1963
Travelled through the USA for three months for *Kristall*.

1964
Joined the photographic staff of the magazine *Stern*.
Went to India, where he photographed the famine, and to South-East Asia.
Other work on Rhodesia (Zimbabwe), the US Marine Corps, Spain and Portugal.

1972
Worked as a cameraman and producer of television documentaries on Washington and Canada.

1973
Two films on the famine in Ethiopia. Helped initiate a rescue operation to the area on behalf of *Stern*.

1974
Worked as a correspondent in the German Democratic Republic (moving to East Berlin for two years), together with his wife Eva Höpker-Windmöller, who had been writing for *Stern* for several years.

1975
Collaborated with Heinz Mack on sculpture/photography project in Algeria and Greenland.

1976
Moved to New York to work with his wife as correspondent for *Stern*.
Travelled to Japan.

1978
Began work as executive editor on the American edition of *Geo* magazine. Responsible for photography and graphics.

1981
Left *Geo*.
Established himself in New York working freelance for various magazines and publishers, mainly *Stern* and *Geo*.

1982
Travelled to Greece, Cuba, California and West Africa.
Began work on a book on the history of the former German colonies and another on New York.

1983
Travelled to Africa, China, New Guinea and South Pacific.

Index of photographs

The photograph on page 35 was taken for a cover of *Stern* magazine in 1977.

First published in 1984 by
William Collins Sons & Co Ltd
London · Glasgow · Sydney
Auckland · Johannesburg

© 1983 Gruppo Editoriale Fabbri S.p.A.,
Milan

ISBN 0 00 411949 4

Typesetting by Chambers Wallace, London
Printed in Italy